Brain Sizzlers

Philip Carter and Ken Russell

Sterling Publishi
New Yo

Book design by Lundquist Design, New York

10 9 8 7 6 5 4 3 2 1

Published 2003 by Sterling Publishing Co., Inc.
387 Park Avenue South, New York, NY 10016
Previously published by Barnes & Noble, Inc.,
under the title *Mighty Mites Deluxe book of Brain Sizzlers* and originally
published in four separate volumes in the *Mighty Mites* series.
Copyright © 2002 by Philip Carter and Ken Russell
Distributed in Canada by Sterling Publishing
℅ Canadian Manda Group, One Atlantic Avenue, Suite 105
Toronto, Ontario, Canada M6K 3E7
Distributed in Great Britain by Chrysalis Books
64 Brewery Road, London N7 9NT, England
Distributed in Australia by Capricorn Link (Australia) Pty. Ltd.
P.O. Box 704, Windsor, NSW 2756, Australia

Printed in China

Sterling ISBN 1-4027-0957-9

Substitute letters for numbers to find five 8-letter words
that are all anagrams of each other:

1 2 3 4 5 6 7 8

4 7 1 8 2 3 5 6

2 8 7 4 1 3 5 6

3 5 1 8 6 2 4 7

4 7 8 2 1 3 5 6

1 Answer

triangle
altering
relating
integral
alerting

In each of the following groups of three words, your task is to choose two of the three that can be combined to form an anagram of another word, which is a synonym of the remaining word. For example, LEG—MEEK—NET. The words LEG and NET are an anagram of GENTLE, which is a synonym of the remaining word MEEK.

> novel — invite — nova
> host — tumult — die
> rebate — toil — erase
> leap — due — bay
> grit — cure — ago
> gave — pied — tirade
> action — coup — trade
> hew — prim — cry
> peg — slim — see
> sip — vow — more
> stem — vent — robe
> nib — asset — crib

2 Answer

novel — innovative

host — multitude

erase — obliterate

due — payable

grit — courage

pied — variegated

trade — occupation

cry — whimper

see — glimpse

vow — promise

robe — vestment

crib — bassinet

Start at the top left-hand corner letter, and move from letter to adjacent letter horizontally, vertically, and diagonally to spell out a familiar phrase. Finish at the bottom right-hand corner letter. Every letter must be used only once.

```
T  H  E  W
T  H  A  Y
S  A  T  C  O  K
T  H  E  O  C  I
      U  R  L  E
      M  B  E  S
```

3 Answer

That's the way the cookie crumbles.

Rearrange the letters to form the names of five countries. Transfer the arrowed letters into the key anagram and then rearrange the letters to form the name of a sixth country.

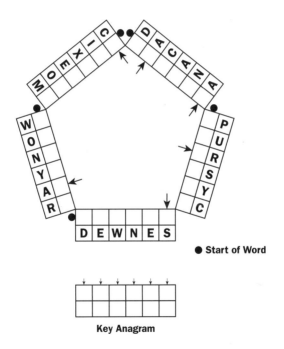

● Start of Word

Key Anagram

4 Answer

Canada
Cyprus
Sweden
Norway
Mexico

Key: Panama

Arrange the following words into three sets of three:

asbestos, asserted, cassette, crescent, ensheath, noisiest, osteitis, prospect, suspects

At a recent school board election a total of 84,962 votes were cast for the four candidates, the winner beating his opponents by 22,896, 42,891, and 48,399 votes respectively.

How many votes were cast for each candidate?

5 Answer

Arrange them so that in each set the word SET appears in the same position:

aSsErTed	caSsEtTe	creScEnT
aSbEsTos	enShEaTh	noiSiEsT
oStEiTis	suSpEcTs	proSpEcT

6 Answer

Add 84,962 + 22,896 + 42,891 + 48,399 = 199,148.
Divide by 4 = 49,787.
49,787 is the number of votes received by the successful candidate.

The second received 49,787 - 22,896 = 26,891.
The third received 49,787 - 42,891 = 6,896.
The fourth received 49,787 - 48,399 = 1,388.

Start by solving the cryptogram that follows, which is a straightforward code in which each letter of the alphabet has been replaced by another.

P RXKII PF ZHI CKDHXIK ZK ZKNK IM DMQVUKFKUJ
XLUPTK PL KXKNJ ZHJ. CXF, UPTK CHDML HLE KRRI, ZK
IKKQKE FM CK HCMXF VKNOKDF FMRKFGKN—CXF LMF
IM RMME HVHNF.
                                —MUPYKN GHNEJ

Now try to find a keyed phrase connected with the cryptogram. Against each letter of plain text (line 1 below) write its encoded form (line 2). Then, against each letter of code text (line 3) write its plain-text form (line 4). You will find that some letters in line 4 are in alphabetical order; the letters that are not are those that make up the key phrase. They appear in their correct order, although, of course, repeated letters have been omitted and must be replaced; for example, ANPLEDY would be all that would appear of "an apple a day."

1. ABCDEFGHIJKLMNOPQRSTUVWXYZ
2.
3. ABCDEFGHIJKLMNOPQRSTUVWXYZ
4.

I guess it was because we were so completely unlike in every way. But, like bacon and eggs, we seemed to be about perfect together — but not so good apart.

— Oliver Hardy

Keyed phrase: That's yet another fine mess.

Find the names of 13 animals in the grid. They can all be
found reading horizontally and vertically (but not
diagonally), backwards or forwards, but always in a straight
line.

```
                  C
               C  A  T
            S  H  R  E  W
         D  O  E  I  G  N  U
      C  O  W  E  B  I  S  O  N
         G  S  T  O  A  T  G
            T  A  U  C  E
               H  O  G
                  S
```

caribou
shrew
cat
cheetah
hog
stoat
bison
teg
gnu
sow
doe
cow
dog

Find a trite saying by arranging the 16 words in the wheel in the correct order.

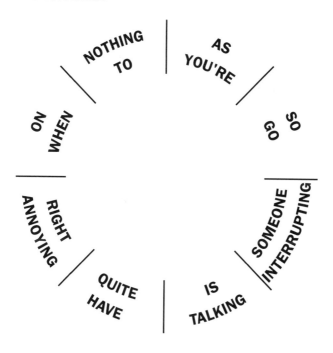

Nothing is quite so annoying as to have someone go right on talking when you're interrupting.

A   B   C   D   E   F   G   H

What letter is two to the right of the letter that is immediately to the right of the letter four to the left of the letter immediately to the right of the letter two to the left of the letter that lies midway between the letter two to the right of the letter F and the letter three to the right of the letter C?

Odd Word Out 11

Which of the following words is the odd one out?

merit	balustrade	baton	continuity
riled	lamentable	laird	paraglider
rated	embittered	unity	deter
bleat	primordial	summertime	

10 Answer

E

11 Answer

Baton. In all the others, one of the 5-letter words is an anagram of the last 5 letters of one of the 10-letter words.

paraglider — riled,   summertime — merit,
continuity — unity,   balustrade — rated,
primordial — laird,   embittered — deter,
lamentable — bleat

Arrange the group of fourteen words in pairs so that each pair is an anagram of another word or name. The seven words produced have a linking theme. For example, if the words TRY and CREASE appeared in the list, they could be paired to form the word SECRETARY, and the theme could be *professions*.

ARC	CANE
DOG	GAP
GENTLE	GONE
LARGE	MATURE
PATH	PIE
SELL	TENON
TIN	ZIP

12 **Answer**

pentagon (gap tenon)
triangle (large tin)
decagon (dog cane)
ellipse (sell pie)
heptagon (gone path)
rectangle (gentle arc)
trapezium (mature zip)

The theme is *geometric shapes*.

In how many of the following will a knot be formed when both ends of the string are pulled simultaneously?

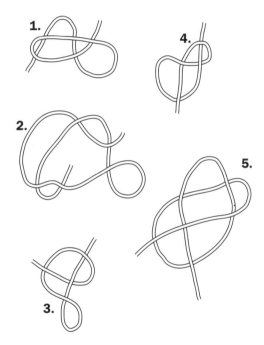

13 Answer

Numbers 3 and 4 will form a knot.

Five consecutive numbers have been hidden in the shapes as indicated by the question marks.

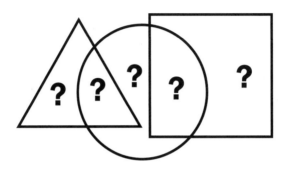

When added together,

The numbers in the triangle = 27
The numbers in the circle = 39
The numbers in the square = 24
The total of all five numbers = 65

What numbers should replace the question marks?

14 **Answer**

triangle: 15 and 12
circle: 12, 14, and 13
square: 13 and 11

Creature Groupies

The names of these animal groups have been listed incorrectly. Rearrange them to match the correct group name with the creatures it describes.

glean of toads

ostentation of raven

paddling of peacocks

parliament of starlings

pod of larks

unkindness of owls

exultation of ducks

knot of whales

erst of herrings

murmuration of bees

Five Ages

The ages of five family members total 100 between them.

Pete and Jodie total 41 between them;
Jodie and Carol total 17 between them;
Carol and Alan total 54 between them;
Alan and Maria total 45 between them.

How old is each family member?

15 Answer

glean of herrings

ostentation of peacocks

paddling of ducks

parliament of owls

pod of whales

starlings

unkindness of ravens

exultation of larks

knot of toads

erst of bees

murmeration of

16 Answer

Pete: 38

Jodie: 3

Carol: 14

Alan: 40

Maria: 5

Find in the grid a 3-by-3 magic square, where the three numbers reading across, down, and from corner to corner all add up to the same total.

2	9	1	6	42	96	12	21
15	3	5	7	19	18	3	14
12	4	8	2	52	5	40	25
81	1	6	9	75	10	15	45
36	32	24	64	6	15	20	30
78	72	40	8	16	72	86	14
10	16	56	48	12	24	27	76
58	36	12	36	96	84	9	13

17 **Answer**

32	24	64
72	40	8
16	56	48

Complete the words so that the last 2 letters of the first word are the first 2 letters of the second word, and the last 2 letters of the second word are the first 2 letters of the third word, etc. The last 2 letters of the tenth word are the first 2 letters of the first word, thus completing the circle.

```
*  *  D U  *  *
*  *  B A  *  *
*  *  M P  *  *
*  *  N G  *  *
*  *  I R  *  *
*  *  P I  *  *
*  *  E A  *  *
*  *  R I  *  *
*  *  J U  *  *
*  *  O L  *  *
```

18 Answer

endure
rebate
temple
length
thirty
typist
steamy
myriad
adjust
stolen

Can you accurately draw the contents of the hexagon with the question mark?

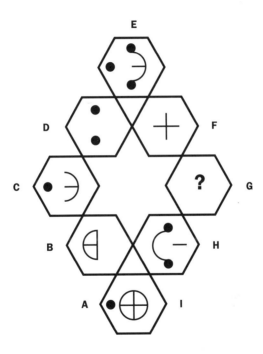

Look along straight lines of three hexagons (A, B, and C, for example).

In that example, B added to A equals C, but like symbols disappear. C added to D equals E, with like symbols disappearing.

Don't Go Bananas! 20

How many different ways can the letters in the word BANANAS be rearranged?

Fair Deal 21

If we take one hundred cards, numbered 1 to 100, what are the chances that if the cards are shuffled and the top six cards dealt out, they would be drawn in ascending order, that is, each card having a higher number than the previous card?

20 Answer

$$\frac{7!}{3 \times 2}$$

or $\dfrac{7 \times 6 \times 5 \times 4 \times 3 \times 2 \times 1}{6} = 840$

21 Answer

We are interested only in the top six cards.
These can be dealt in series in 720 different ways.

i.e., 1 x 2 x 3 x 4 x 5 x 6 = 720 or 6!
The chances are, therefore, 1 in 720, or 719 to 1.

Find the starting point and spiral clockwise to find a familiar phrase. Only alternate letters are shown.

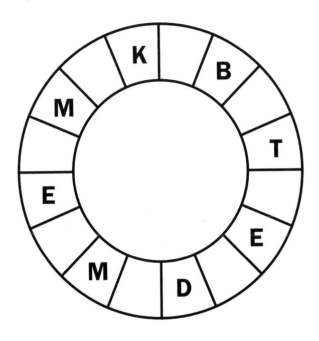

Make both ends meet.

Which of the following phrases is the odd one out?

Jack-in-the-box
magnetic flux
notary public
talcum powder
flying saucer
absolute zero
house-warming
mothers-in-law
staying power
thunder claps

absolute zero

None of the others repeats a letter.

13	14	12	1
2	11	7	6
3	10	16	15
8	5	9	4

The above is an antimagic square where none of the horizontal, vertical, or corner-to-corner lines add up to 34. By changing the position of just four of the numbers, however, it is possible to make a perfect magic square where each horizontal, vertical, and corner-to-corner line adds up to 34.

Which four numbers should be swapped?

13	**8**	12	1
2	11	7	**14**
3	10	**6**	15
16	5	9	4

Insert the 26 letters of the alphabet into the grid only once each, to complete the crossword. Seven letters have already been placed for you.

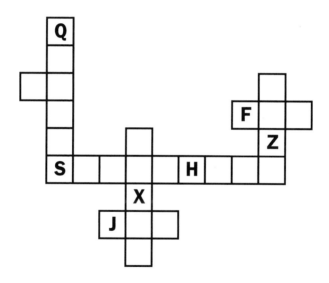

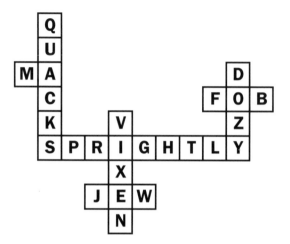

Divide the square into four segments of identical size and shape so that each segment contains one each of the four different symbols.

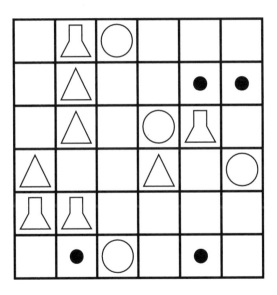

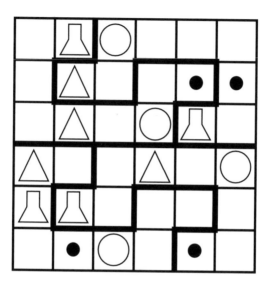

Find a 12-letter word by finding the starting point and moving from letter to letter around the circumference and across chords. Letters that are only one, two, or three letters away from each other are connected along the circumference; letters that are four or more letters away from each other are connected by chords.

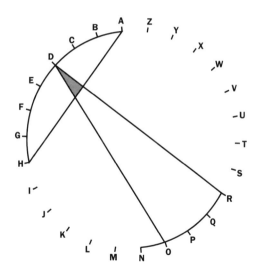

27 Answer

dodecahedron

Find a 10-letter word by moving from circle to adjacent circle along the connecting lines. All letters are used only once each.

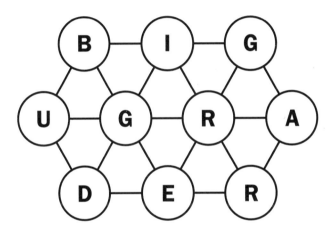

.28 **Answer**

budgerigar

In a horse race, a bookmaker offered odds on the five runners as follows:

Peanut Vendor	16-1 against
Moonlight Serenade	2-1 against
Melancholy Baby	?
Unforgettable	4-1 against
Lazy River	5-1 against
Pennies From Heaven	9-1 against

What odds should the bookmaker offer on Melancholy Baby to produce a 10 percent profit if he balanced his books?

3-1 against

Assessment as follows (stake on each horse to win $100):

		$
Peanut Vendor	16-1	6
Moonlight Serenade	2-1	33
Melancholy Baby	3-1	25
Unforgettable	4-1	20
Lazy River	5-1	16
Pennies from Heaven	9-1	10
		110

110 = total staked to win 100 (10 percent profit)

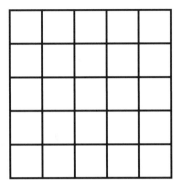

Complete the magic square with five 5-letter words so that each 5-letter word can be read both horizontally and vertically. Clues are provided below (in no particular order):

cord with weight for entangling an animal
workers available for employment
becomes conscious
transparent substance used in varnishes
giraffelike African animal

30 Answer

L	A	B	O	R
A	W	O	K	E
B	O	L	A	S
O	K	A	P	I
R	E	S	I	N

Spell out two related words by starting at one of the hexagons and selecting a letter. Then choose another hexagon that includes the same letter you have chosen, and select another letter. Keep repeating the process to spell out your two related words, one 9 letters long and the other 5 letters long. Each hexagon is visited at least twice on your travels.

For example, by starting at hexagon 3 it is possible to spell out the word CLOVER in this way by visiting hexagons 3, 2, 3, 1, 3, and 2 in turn.

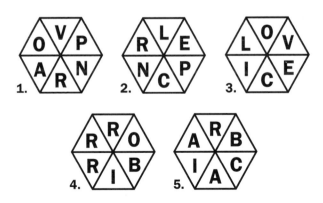

31 **Answer**

Capricorn and Libra, by visiting hexagons
2, 5, 1, 2, 4, 5, 3, 4, 1 2, 3, 5, 4, and 5 in turn.

Solve each clue to find seven words, each containing the letters SIN.

SIN*****	freedom from hypocrisy
*SIN****	mica
SIN*	advise badly
SIN	with humor
****SIN**	former name of Ethiopia
*****SIN*	luxurious sedan
******SIN	birthplace of Spencer Tracy and Orson Welles

7
84
951
?
3

What number is missing?

32 Answer

sincerity
isinglass
misinform
amusingly
Abyssinia
limousine
Wisconsin

33 Answer

620.
Read diagonally from left to right, top to bottom on a standard calculator keypad:

7	8	9
4	5	6
1	2	3
0		

What number should replace the question mark?

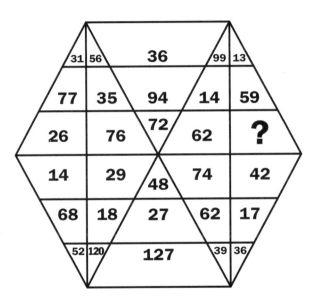

23.

The total of the three numbers in each section at the top is the same as the total of the three numbers in the opposite mirror image section in the bottom half.

For example: $36 + 94 + 72 = 48 + 27 + 127$.

Using the following letters, complete the magic square below so that the five words read the same both across and down.

B B B C G L M M R R S S

	A		O	
A		O		A
	O		E	
O		E		A
	A		A	

C	A	R	O	B
A	R	O	M	A
R	O	B	E	S
O	M	E	G	A
B	A	S	A	L

All of the vowels have been omitted from this trite saying.
How quickly can you replace them and uncover the saying?

FYTLL THBSS YWRLT FRWRK BCSYH DFLTT
YRTHN XTMRN NGYWL LHVFL TTYR.

Can you decode the message below?

PRIA CHCN PIAX ZOCR TDOV
XMUH JGBK MYCK
MTEA CHKD FJSA CVTN PQVH
JSTR TSBS UDCD
FORQ SIEN PACT VTUR TOLM

36 **Answer**

If you tell the boss you were late for work because you had a flat tyre, the next morning you will have a flat tyre.

37 **Answer**

Boys will be boisterous.

Read the missing letters between each group of four.

For example:
PRIA **B** CHCN **O** PIAX **Y** ZOCR.

With what value weight must you replace the question mark in order to balance the scales?

6 lbs.   8 lbs.   9 lbs. **?**

38 **Answer**

4 lbs.

left	right
6 lbs. x 6 = 36	9 lbs. x 4 = 36
8 lbs. x 3 = <u>24</u>	4 lbs. x 6 = <u>24</u>
60	60

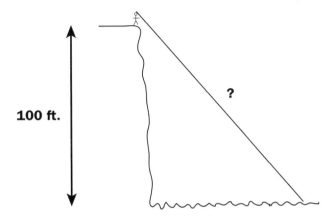

100 ft.

?

If you are standing on the top of a 100-foot-high cliff looking out to sea on a clear day, how far would you be able to see?

12.25 miles

There is a formula for working this out, which is:

$$\text{HEIGHT} = \frac{2n^2}{3} \text{ feet}$$

where n equals the distance in miles.

Therefore, in this instance,

$$100 = \frac{2n^2}{3}, \text{ therefore } 300 = 2n^2$$

and $150 = n^2$.

n = square root of 150, which is 12.25.

Insert the numbers 0-8 in the circles, so that for any particular circle, the sum of the numbers in the circles connected directly to it equals the value of the number in the circle as given in the list.

For Example

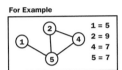

1 = 5
2 = 9
4 = 7
5 = 7

$$0 = 13$$
$$1 = 19$$
$$2 = 11$$
$$3 = 1$$
$$4 = 17$$
$$5 = 8$$
$$6 = 4$$
$$7 = 8$$
$$8 = 4$$

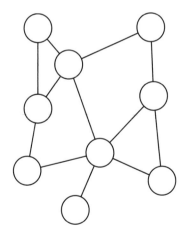

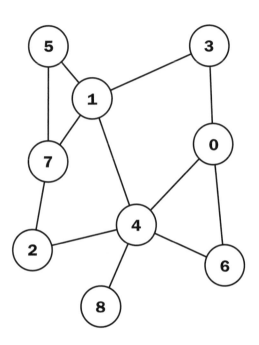

Find sixteen 6-letter words by pairing up the thirty-two 3-letter bits in the target.

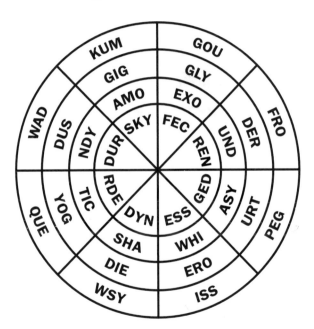

kumiss

exodus

dynamo

pegged

render

giggly

gourde

whisky

waddie

frowsy

fecund

shandy

duress

queasy

yogurt

exotic

Which five of the six pieces below can be fitted together to form a perfect square?

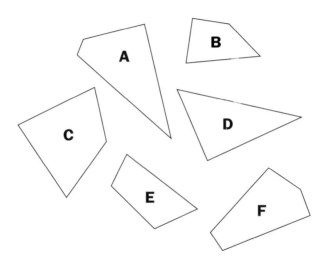

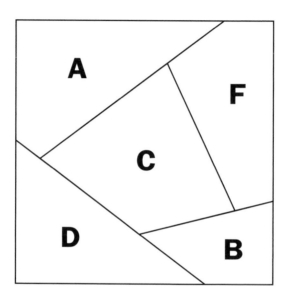

Carry on the series by replacing the question mark.

3
13
1113
3113
132113
?

Which one of these words is the odd one out?

united
badly
twenty
leeward
docile
practice

43 Answer

1113122113

The digits describe the previous set.
132113 is literally, one 1, one 3, one 2,
two 1, one 3.

44 Answer

united
All the other words have an aquatic creature carried in
the word reading backward:

(bad)ly—dab
(twen)ty—newt
(lee)ward—eel
(doc)ile—cod
(prac)tice—carp

What number should replace the question mark?

```
    1        0        8   2              5   5
 1              2   1            4    1             8
    5        8        9   6              8   ?
```

50^3 divided by $50^2 = 50^1 = 50$.
50^2 multiplied by $50^2 = 50^4 = 6,250,000$.

What is the value of 50^0?

45 **Answer**

2

58 x 19 = 1,102, 96 x 19 = 1,824,
82 x 19 = 1,558

46 **Answer**

1

Any number to the zero power (indices) is 1.
The proof of this is: 50^3 divided by 50^3 = 1
With indices, *divided by* means taken away *multiplied by* means added together. So, 50^3 divided by 50^3 = 50^0 = 1.

One man can paint a fence in 2 hours.
One man can paint a fence in 3 hours.
One man can paint a fence in 4 hours.
One man can paint a fence in 5 hours.
One man can paint a fence in 6 hours.

If they all worked at their respective rates, how long would
they take to paint the fence all working together?

What number should replace the question mark?

1	7	7	6
4	7	5	8
3	8	3	4
2	9	9	?

47 Answer

It is necessary to take reciprocals to solve this
problem, so each number of hours is divided into 1.
2 = .5
3 = .333
4 = .25
5 = .2
6 = .167
   1.45
Then you must take the reciprocal again:
$\frac{1}{1.45}$ = .7 hours, or approximately 40 minutes.

48 Answer

4.
Each pair of numbers on the left is doubled to
produce the numbers on the right (in no particular
order)
17 x 2 = 34
47 x 2 = 94
38 x 2 = 76
29 x 2 = 58

A quotation has been divided into 3-letter chunks (ignoring punctuation and spaces). Each chunk is then arranged in alphabetical order for you to rearrange correctly.

For example, *Find the quote* would be FIN DTH EQU OTE. Alphabetically it would be DTH EQU FIN OTE. The numbers tell you how many letters are in each word of the quotation. The asterisks represent capitalized words, in this case the name of the author.

1, 8, 2, 2, 5, 2, 2, 4, *6, *7

ACE	AHO	AMU	CKS	ELG
ESI	ISN	OLD	OPL	SPI
TAL	TOB	WYN		

A hospital is no place to be sick.
                    —Samuel Goldwyn

What familiar phrase is indicated below?

If half of 5 is 3, what is one-third of 10?

50 Answer

broken promises

51 Answer

4

If 2.5 = 3
then, (x 4) 10 = 12
and 1/3 x 10 = 12/3
then 1/3 of 10 = 4.

2496

19

3827   16

24   5981
        17   7629

What number should replace the question mark?

3814   23

        7246   ?

8817   21

        20   5228

24

All the two-figure numbers in the bottom group are the sums of the digits of all the four-figure numbers in the top group, and vice versa.

Which two letters, when they replace the question marks, will complete six words if you use the letters on the left only once each to start the words and the letters on the right only once each to complete them?

```
      L        M                    S
           C              ??   D         U
        B    G
   D                          Y    E    T
```

Who is the Greatest? 54

The Pharoah asked "who is the greatest of the gods?"

"I am not," said Horus

"Anubis is," said Isis

"Isis is lying," said Anubis

Only one of the gods was telling the truth, the other two were lying.

Who is the greatest of the gods?

53 Answer

EN

The words formed are menu, bend, cent, deny, gene, and lens.

54 Answer

Horus.

The animals are kept in the following cages
at the zoo:

lions	47
tigers	58
elephants	87
parrots	69

What is the cage number of the sealions?

Five pool balls are placed in a row. What ball is two to the
left of the ball that is immediately to the right of the ball
that is two to the right of the ball that is three to the left of
the ball that is immediately to the right of the ball that is
two less in value than the ball which is three to the right of
the ball two to the left of the 5-ball?

55 Answer

72

Consonants are valued 11 and vowels 7:

S	=	11
E	=	7
A	=	7
L	=	11
I	=	7
O	=	7
N	=	11
S	=	<u>11</u>
		72

56 Answer

The 3-ball.

What are the chances of drawing out of a standard pack of fifty-two playing cards the following cards in the order shown?

first   King of Hearts
second   King of Spades
third   King of Diamonds
fourth   King of Clubs

The cards are not replaced after drawing.

What is the missing letter?

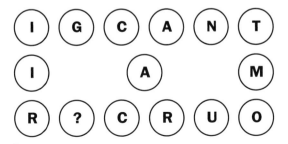

57 **Answer**

$$\frac{1}{52} \times \frac{1}{51} \times \frac{1}{50} \times \frac{1}{49}$$

$$= \frac{1}{6,497,400}$$

58 **Answer**

V

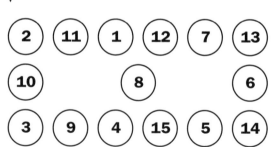

Follow the route shown, jumping to alternate letters to spell out the word circumnavigator.

The five cog wheels are in contact with each other. The number of cogs on each wheel is as indicated on each wheel. How many revolutions must be made before all of the cogs are returned to their original start positions?

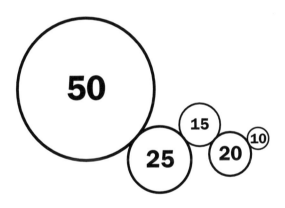

12 revolutions

This type of puzzle is solved by first taking the lowest common multiple (LCM), or the lowest number that all five cog numbers will divide into.

The lowest common multiple is 600. This is then divided by the largest wheel.
So $\frac{600}{50}$ = 12 revolutions.

In each of the following a familiar phrase has had 1 letter altered in each of its words, and the words have then been put in the wrong order. Can you find the phrases? For example HOLD ON TIGHT might be MIGHT BOLD IN.

tone ball tie

i ban blond at

do i heal some

share is wood

any tall miss

due sever may

cops prod any

pay allen tip

on moss sit

call the tune
blind as a bat
come to a head
in good shape
kiss and tell
never say die
pros and cons
Tin Pan alley
hit or miss

Find a word and its container for each of the clues below.
For example: vegetable in a weapon (3 in 5)
Answer: s(pea)r

leporine creatures in a capital city (5 in 9)
man of refinement in a South American
    country (4 in 9)
finish in a ranch house (3 in 8)
capital city in a constellation (4 in 9)
seabird in a bone (4 in 7)
monkey in a polygon (3 in 9)
rodents in pasta (4 in 10)
heavenly ring in an octopus (4 in 10)
film star in a fish dish (4 in 8)

Buc(hares)t
Ar(gent)ina
haci(end)a
And(rome)da
s(tern)um
tr(ape)zium
ver(mice)lli
cep(halo)pod
ked(gere)e

Find the smallest number that will divide by the nine digits
1, 2, 3, 4, 5, 6, 7, 8, and 9 and leave no remainder.

Start at the letter in the top left-hand corner and work from
letter to adjacent letter horizontally, vertically, or diagonally to
spell out a trite saying known as Knight's Law. You must use
each letter once each only and finish at the bottom right-hand
square.

L	E	F	A	O	Y	E
I	I	H	T	U	L	R
S	W	H	H	I	A	E
P	A	U	W	K	A	M
E	P	O	I	H	E	R
N	Y	O	N	T	L	P
S	T	G	O	A	N	S

62 **Answer**

2520, which is 5 x 7 x 8 x 9.

63 **Answer**

Life is what happens to you while you are making other plans.

Start at the asterisk (✳) and move from letter to adjacent letter by moving horizontally, vertically, and diagonally to spell out six words that are similar in meaning. Each letter must be used, but only once. Finish at the bottom right-hand corner.

C	T	H	P	B	I	L
H	I	R	O	U	U	A
R	I	O	E	J	J	N
L	D	V	✳	D	T	O
E	L	J	E	H	E	Y
E	O	R	E	T	G	F
Y	D	D	L	I	U	L

euphoric
thrilled
overjoyed
delighted
jubilant
joyful

Find the two hexagons below that are the odd ones out from the rest.

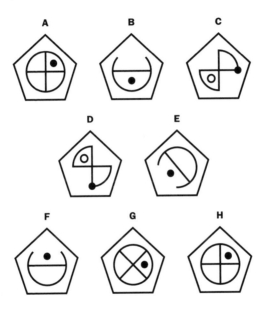

65 **Answer**

G and B.

C and D; A and H; and E and F are the same figures.

Cryptogram 66

Decode the following, which is a straightforward substitution cryptogram in which each letter of the alphabet has been replaced by another.

JMC KYJWHWZT YQKPBLWHZ XC BWEC
WT JMC GCZJ KU LBB YKZZWGBC
XKQBRZ; LTR JMC YCZZWHWZJ UCLQZ
JMWZ WZ JQVC.

FLHCZ G PLGCBB

Odd One Out 67

Which word is the odd one out?

ceremonial   accusatory

disallowed

enthusiasm   statuesque   girlfriend

disuniting

66 **Answer**

The optimist proclaims we
live in the best of all
possible worlds; and the
pessimist fears this is
true.

James B. Cabell

67 **Answer**

Disallowed.
They all have an abbreviation for a day of the week
embedded within the word—for example girl(fri)end;
however, disallo(wed) has the abbreviation at the end,
not in the middle.

Age-Old Problem 68

The combined age of Frasier and Daphne is 146 years.
The combined age of Daphne and Tom is 154 years.
The combined age of Frasier and Tom is 156 years.

Figure out each person's age.

Find the Sequence 69

What number *completes* the sequence below.

9, 16, 18, 22, 24, 27, 30, ?

68 **Answer**

Frasier is 74.
Daphne is 72.
Tom is 82.

69 **Answer**

32.

The numbers represent the numerical
position of all the letter Es in the question.

Find the longest word that can be spelled out by moving from letter to adjacent letter horizontally, vertically, and diagonally, but not repeating a letter.

X	G	A	J	Y
K	N	V	B	P
C	D	L	R	F
E	H	I	T	U
M	W	S	O	Q

70 **Answer**

disturbance

Find a Trite Saying

Rearrange the words below to find a trite saying.

RAIN	THEN	FAIR	BACK
A	LEND	TO	IT
STARTS	WHEN	UMBRELLA	YOU
THEY	IS	AN	ASK
IN	WEATHER	FOR	BANK
PLACE	IT	WHERE	A

Critters

What do these creatures have in common?

> guinea pig
> jack rabbit
> silk worm
> firefly
> prairie dog

71 **Answer**

A bank is a place where they lend you an umbrella in fair weather, then ask for it back when it starts to rain.

72 **Answer**

None are what they seem from their names.
The Guinea pig is a rodent, not a pig;
The jack rabbit is a hare not a rabbit;
The silk worm is a caterpillar not a worm;
The firefly is a beetle not a fly;
The prairie dog is a rodent not a dog.

Which day is two days before the day immediately
following the day three days before the day four days after
the day two days after the day three days before the day
immediately before Thursday?

In the span of one year, each cat in the rat-infested state of
Catattackya killed the same number of rats as every other
cat. The total number of rat fatalities during the year came
to 1,111,111.

Less than 500 cats achieved this remarkable feat.
How many cats were there in Catattackya? And how many
rats did each kill?

73 Answer

Tuesday.

74 Answer

239 cats. Each caught 4,649 rats.
1,111,111 = 239 x 4,649. Both of these factors
are prime.

Each of the following is an anagram of a familiar phrase.

glad nag croaked (5-3-6)

free heath roll (4-3-7)

lands buttons (4, 3, 5)

swan forever (3, 2, 6)

heat it on kitchen (4, 2, 2, 3, 4)

75 Answer

cloak-and-dagger
hell-for-leather
nuts and bolts
war of nerves
take it on the chin

Two 3-digit numbers not containing zeros are exactly equal to the sum of the cubes of their three digits. Find them. For example, allowing zeros, the number 407 meets this criteria:

$$4^3 = 64$$
$$0^3 = 0$$
$$7^3 = \underline{343}$$
$$407$$

Find another 3-digit number with a zero that meets this criteria.

Solve the anagrams in brackets (word lengths are given), to complete the quotation by Alice Roosevelt Longworth:

The (free cost) (the royal tune) is (revealed deportments).
     6,2   7,5   8,11

76 **Answer**

153 and 371.

370.

77 **Answer**

The secret of eternal youth is arrested development.

Using all 25 letters of the following phrase only once each, find five 5-letter words that, when fit into the grid, will form a magic square in which the same five words can be read both horizontally and vertically:

RETAIN ONE SESSION NEW JESTER

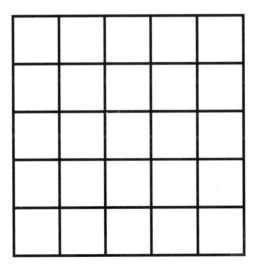

J	O	I	S	T
O	W	N	E	R
I	N	A	N	E
S	E	N	S	E
T	R	E	E	S

What do the initials stand for?
For example: 4 W on an A is 4 **w**heels on an **a**utomobile.

    37 DCBT in H
    6 F on a C
    The 7 F of DL
    12 L in the HA
    3 is a GB on the BS
    10 Y in a D
    5 L in a L
    640 A in a SM
    3 P in a G of H
    7 S on a H

37 degrees centigrade body temperature in humans
6 faces on a cube
The 7 Faces of Dr. Lao
12 letters in the Hawaiian alphabet
3 is a gentle breeze on the Beaufort Scale
10 years in a decade
5 lines in a limerick
640 acres in a square mile
3 periods in a game of hockey
7 sides on a heptagon

A Perfect Union 80

Arrange the numbers **1, 2, 3, 4, 5, 6, 7, 8, 9, 0** into two separate fractions that make unity (1) when added together. Use each number only once.

Key to the Answer 81

Find the unusual connection between these words.

    flask
    flash
    flags

When you have found the connection, find as many 4-letter words as you can that display the same feature.

80 **Answer**

$$\frac{35}{70} + \frac{148}{296} = \frac{1}{2} + \frac{1}{2} = 1$$

81 **Answer**

If you use each key once, they are the longest common words that can be typed on the middle row of a typewriter or computer keyboard.

4-letter words that can be typed on the middle row are dash, flag, flak, glad, half, lads, lash, slag, gash, hags, lags, fads, and jags.

Find the number that comes next in this sequence.

355
410
425
440
?

Add two Es to the following group of letters to form another English word. The order of the letters can be changed around as you wish.

far

82 **Answer**

455.

The numbers are clock times, without the colon, with 15 minutes added each time:

3:55
4:10
4:25
4:40
4:55

83 **Answer**

software.

far + two Es = software

Each letter in this multiplication problem represents a different digit.

$$\begin{array}{r} \text{snore} \\ \underline{\times \quad \text{y}} \\ \text{zzzzzz} \end{array}$$

Solve each of the anagrams to complete a quotation by Lily Tomlin.

--- -------- -------- -- -------

mind an event   **against faulty egos**

--- ---- ---- -- --------

denied sheep   **calm option**

84 **Answer**

```
  95238
    x 7
 666666
```

85 **Answer**

Man invented language to satisfy his deep
need to complain.

Find the number that should replace the question mark.

```
  4    7              1    4              4    6
6   10    2        3   11    2        8    ?    4
  8    9              8    7              7    8
```

The following is a straightforward cryptogram where each letter of the alphabet has been substituted by another:

NAYI P NWR W QAPTC, BU BVFAYD RWPC FV

BY, "PJ UVM LYQVBY W RVTCPYD UVM'TT LY W

ZYIYDWT. PJ UVM LYQVBY W BVIG UVM'TT YIC

MK WR FAY KVKY." PIRFYWC P LYQWBY W

KWPIFYD WIC NVMIC MK WR KPQWRRV.

KWLTV KPQWRRV

86 **Answer**

9.

In each group, opposite digits are subtracted and the three answers added to arrive at the number in the middle.

Thus: 8 - 4 = 4
          8 - 4 = 4
          7 - 6 = <u>1</u>
                    9

87 **Answer**

When I was a child, my mother said to me, "If you become a soldier you'll be a general. If you become a monk you'll end up as the pope." Instead I became a painter and wound up as Picasso.

Pablo Picasso

To complete the crossword, substitute letters for numbers from the choices given in the key.

[1] 2	■	[2] 1	3	[3] 7	[4] 2	■
[5] 5	1	6	■	[6] 5	8	[7] 4
2	■	[8] 1	3	6	2	2
[9] 6	[10] 1	5	■	[11] 6	6	9
[12] 3	7	3	2	2	■	2
[13] 2	6	1	■	[14] 2	7	2
■	[15] 1	4	7	5	■	5

Key:

1	2	3	4	5	6	7	8	9
A	D	G	J	M	P	S	V	Y
B	E	H	K	N	Q	T	W	Z
C	F	I	L	O	R	U	X	

88 Answer

E		C	I	T	E	
M	A	R		O	W	L
E		A	G	R	E	E
R	A	N		P	R	Y
G	U	I	D	E		D
E	R	A		D	U	E
	A	L	S	O		N

If we presented you with the words MAR, FAR, and AM, and asked you to produce the shortest word in the English language that contained the letters from which only these words can be produced, we would expect you to come up with the word FARM.

Here is a second list of words:

BRIDAL, PEDANTIC, CAPTURED, LARCENY

What is the shortest word containing only the letters from which these four words can be produced?

89 Answer

Unpredictably.

Solve the five clues, enter the answers in the pyramid, and then rearrange all the letters to find a 15-letter word.

1. one thousand
2. Michigan
3. transgress
4. operatic piece
5. frequent as a ghost

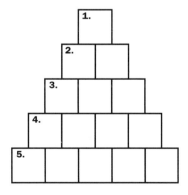

M
MI
SIN
ARIA
HAUNT

15-letter word: HUMANITARIANISM

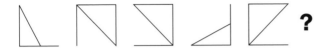

What comes next in the above sequence?

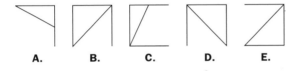

B.

The first three figures of the sequence are being repeated, but are being rotated 90 degrees counterclockwise.

Each horizontal and vertical line contains the jumbled letters of a type of fruit. Find the 16 fruits. Each letter in the grid can be used only once.

```
R  A  A  A  B  N  P  N  U  A
N  P  A  R  A  M  M  I  G  O
E  G  N  N  N  I  P  F  C  E
R  P  E  E  P  L  E  A  N  N
G  A  R  C  H  E  E  E  P  M
A  A  U  M  L  L  P  Q  O
T  W  E  P  O  E  A  O  E  D
P  U  O  U  N  I  A  V  T  L
E  A  G  H  D  C  Y  R  I  R
M  W  N  U  S  P  I  L  P  K
```

Across: banana, mango, fig, pear, peach, plum, date, nut, cherry, pumpkin.
Down: grape, pawpaw, orange, prune, damson, lime, apple, olive, quince, melon/lemon.

Vertical letters used are shown in bold type:

R A **A** A B N **P** N U A
N **P** A **R** **A** M M **I** G O
E G **N** **N** I P F **C** **E**
R **P** **E** **E** P **L** E A **N**
G A **R** C H **E** E **E** P **M**
A **A** U M **M** L **L** P **Q** **O**
T **W** **E** P **O** E A **O** E D
P U **O** U N **I** A V T **L**
E **A** **G** H **D** C Y R **I** R
M **W** N U **S** P I **L** P K

Find out which letters replace the question marks.

A	E	F	L	K	J	T
J	K	L	F	E	A	Y
T	Y	A	E	F	L	K
L	F	E	A	Y	T	J
K	J	T	?	?	E	F
E	A	Y	?	?	K	L
F	L	K	J	T	Y	A

Y A
T J

Starting at the top left-hand corner and
traveling along the top line, then back along
the second line, then along the third line, and
so forth, the letters AEFLKJTY repeat in the
same sequence.

Use all of the letters of the following words only once each to spell out the names of four U.S. cities.

elegant tenable civil servant doodle

If: 1 + 12 = 13
      2 + 9 = 11
      3 + 14 = 17
and 5 + 6 = 11,

then what number do you have to add to 7 so that all these calculations have a rather unusual feature in common?

94 Answer

Cleveland, Galveston, Detroit, and Abilene.

95 Answer

7.

All the calculations are numerically and verbally correct.
7 + 7 = 14 and *seven plus seven* has 14 letters.

Insert the missing numbers so that the calculations are correct, both across and down. All numbers to be inserted are less than 10. Zero is not used.

1	+	2	−	3	=	4 8
+	■	X	■	X	■	−
5	−		+	2	=	
÷	■	−	■	−	■	+
6	+	9	÷		=	
=	■	=	■	=	■	=
7 3	X		÷		=	

¹5	+	²6	−	³3	=	⁴8
+		x		x		−
⁵4	−	3	+	2	=	3
÷		−		−		+
⁶3	+	9	÷	3	=	4
=		=		=		=
⁷3	x	9	÷	3	=	9

Solve the four 1-word anagrams below:

> AIRING OF TACIT
> NOTED ROAD
> VIOLET CANNON
> NICE TENT MOP

Now fit each word in its correct place in the quotation below:

The _____ view serves to protect us from the painful job of thinking. *J. K. Galbraith*

Instant _____ takes too long. *Carrie Fisher*

Equal opportunity means everyone will have a fair chance at being _____. *Laurence J. Peter*

Success is a great _____. *Elizabeth Taylor*

conventional (violet cannon)
gratification (airing of tact)
incompetent (nice tent mop)
deodorant (noted road)

PAINT
NEVER
TEXAS
INLAY
BACON

From the following list, select the word that continues the sequence given above.

dance, ideal, Benin, human, juror

Human.

The middle letters of each word are Roman numerals in ascending value: I, V, X, L, C, M.

Find the letter that should replace the question mark.

T	C	H	O
A	O	T	K
S	I	T	E
H	C	E	R
W	U	A	M
?	B	T	L
H	E	E	S

Y.

Start at the top left-hand letter and work to the bottom right-hand letter by jumping from the first to the third letter of each row. Now return to the top left but jump from the second to the fourth letter of each row. You will find the phrase: That's the way the cookie crumbles.

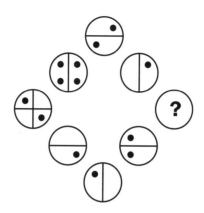

Which circle below should replace the one with the question mark?

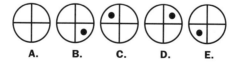

A.   B.   C.   D.   E.

E.

Look along rows of three circles in any direction. You will find that the contents of the third circle in each row is determined by merging the contents of the previous two circles, except that like symbols disappear.

The following words have something in common. What is it?

adjoin

attend

indeed

creamy

astute

The second, fourth, and sixth letters of each word spell out a name. Don, Ted, Ned, Ray, and Sue.

Track the connecting lines from letter to letter to spell out a 14-letter word.

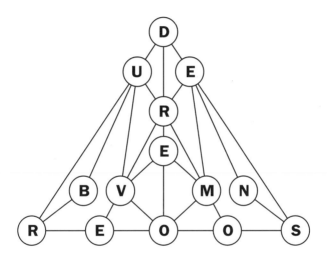

Overburdensome.

Three brothers all started on the same day at different colleges. Jack comes home every 5 days, Marcus comes home every 4 days, and Frank comes home every 3 days. Each one returns to college after just one day.

In how many days will they all be home at the same time?

What number should replace the question mark?

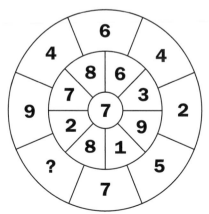

103 Answer

In 60 days.

60 is the lowest common multiple of
5, 4, and 3.

104 Answer

7.
So that looking clockwise the sum of the numbers
formed by the central digit, plus the two adjacent
digits in the middle ring, plus the adjacent digit on
the outer ring, increase by 1 each time starting at 7 + 6
+ 3 + 4 = 20.

Complete the two linked squares by finding two sets of five
5-letter words that will read the same horizontally and
vertically in each grid.

The clues for each grid are given in no particular order.

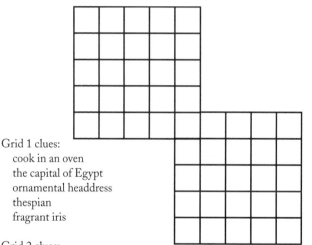

Grid 1 clues:
  cook in an oven
  the capital of Egypt
  ornamental headdress
  thespian
  fragrant iris

Grid 2 clues:
  type of beer
  flat board supported by legs
  at right angles to the length of an aircraft
  abrasive board used for polishing or smoothing
  light-brown color

A	C	T	O	R				
C	A	I	R	O				
T	I	A	R	A				
O	R	R	I	S				
R	O	A	S	T	A	B	L	E
				A	B	E	A	M
				B	E	I	G	E
				L	A	G	E	R
				E	M	E	R	Y

What do all of the following have in common?

a total eclipse

a pig in a poke

white admirals

What is the longest word that can be spelled out by moving from letter to adjacent letter vertically, horizontally, or diagonally and not repeating a letter?

T	P	L	M	W
Q	B	X	Y	H
C	U	A	S	I
K	O	N	R	D
V	G	F	E	J

106 Answer

They all contain the hidden name of a drink.

a tot(al e)clipse
a pi(g in) a poke
whi(te a)dmirals

107 Answer

considerably

5632   4821
                2516

2861   9743

Find the number below that is the odd one out.

        4973   1842

2748   6812   1562

        2356

2748.

Each of the other numbers in the bottom group is paired with a number in the top group that has the same four digits.

CGO

AWA

PFI

ARA

TBU

?

What three letters continue the above sequence?

GTW.

They are the first letters of the signs of the
Zodiac in the order in which they appear
through the year, followed by the first two
letters of what they represent.

Capricorn—goat
Aquarius—water bearer
Pisces—fish
Aries—ram
Taurus—bull
Gemini—twins

Assume both taps in a basin were left on full but with the plug out. The hot-water tap fills the basin in 36 seconds; the cold-water tap fills the basin in 30 seconds; and the plug will release a basin full of water in 24 seconds.

To the nearest second, how long did it take the basin to fill up and overflow, if ever?

Missing Figure 111

What figure is missing?

110 **Answer**

It overflowed in 51 seconds.

36 seconds = 0.6 minutes.
Take the reciprocal $\left(\frac{1}{0.6}\right)$ 1.67

30 seconds = 0.5 minutes,
reciprocal $\left(\frac{1}{0.5}\right)$ 2.00
Added together =   3.67

24 seconds = 0.4 minutes,
reciprocal $\left(\frac{1}{0.4}\right)$ 2.50
Deducted from total =   1.17

The reciprocal of
1.17 $\left(\frac{1}{1.17}\right)$ = 0.85 minutes = 51 seconds.

111 **Answer**

A.
They are the integers 1, 2, 3, 4, 5, 6 drawn complete
with mirror image.

Place all of the following words into the grid to make a crossword.

across	down
notes	nasal
risen	hotel
petal	rated
dates	rites
dosed	mused
hated	doted
roses	noses
betel	deter
nut	per
red	ten

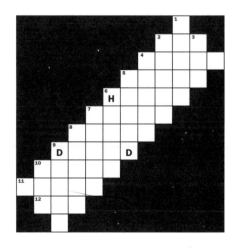

Exchange five of the numbers in the left grid with five of the numbers in the right grid to form two magic-number squares in which each horizontal, vertical, and corner-to-corner line add up to the same total.

17	5	12	20	13
16	23	14	8	4
11	7	25	6	21
2	24	18	9	1
19	10	22	3	15

15	4	20	16	1
2	19	18	23	3
21	10	6	7	11
5	9	14	13	24
22	8	25	13	17

113 Answer

17	5	10	20	13
16	23	14	8	4
11	7	1	25	21
2	24	18	9	12
19	6	22	3	15

15	4	20	16	10
2	19	18	23	3
21	25	1	7	11
5	9	14	13	24
22	8	12	6	17

Arrange these words into four groups of three words each to form new words.

beg, fat, fact, feat
he, her, less, male
one, or, red, woe

BMA LELT TIL ADA HY ***

What three letters come next?

114 **Answer**

Arrange them in groups that spell out four words: feathered, malefactor, woebegone, fatherless.

For example, feat + he + red = feathered

115 **Answer**

RAM – so that when read backwards the sentence: *Mary had a little lamb* appears.

Solve the rebuses below to find three familiar phrases.

    1) time soon

    2) . . . ract . . .

    3) rely vs trust

    First of all
    Starting block
    A fifth of scotch
    The end of the world
    The beginning of the end
    Starting friction
    The middle of the night

What comes next?
    Next of kin
    The middle of nowhere
    Two of a kind
    Second in command
    The start of something big

116 Answer

1) mixed emotions
2) center of attraction
3) hope against hope

117 Answer

The middle of nowhere

Each describes successive letters of the alphabet:
First of **a**ll
Starting **b**lock
A fifth of scot**c**h
The end of the worl**d**
The beginning of the **e**nd
Starting **f**riction
The middle of the ni**g**ht
The middle of now**h**ere

Find a short hidden message in the list of words below.

admire	revive	safari	arched	reason
indigo	adored	rocket	potato	around
anchor	trance	matrix	equate	oyster
esteem	shriek	animal	accuse	report
adverb	effigy	waited	option	picnic
soften	happen	object	bikini	travel
corona	legacy	bureau	tailor	sonata
rabbit	spring	nephew	fiasco	carrot

Starting with the last word of the bottom row and always moving right to left, look at pairs of words. Taking the first and last letters *from these pairs* the message is as follows:

CONGRATULATIONS CODE BREAKER EXTRAORDINAIRE.

For example: **c**arrot and fiasc**o**.

On a chessboard, a knight can move one square horizontally and two vertically, or two horizontally and one vertically. On a 3-by-3 board, the knight can make a maximum of two moves without crossing itself by starting at the top left-hand square and moving as shown.

By starting at the same top left-hand corner, what is the maximum number of moves that the knight can make on a 5-by-5 board without crossing itself?

What is the maximum number of moves it can make on a 6-by-6 board, this time by starting at a square of your choice, but not a corner square?

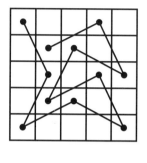 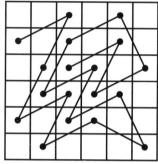

10 moves on the 5-by-5 board;
17 moves on the 6-by-6 board.

Find the number that does not fit.

10234   21672   27669

      15652   17458

   25284   23779   20769

29498   13846

27669.

In all the other numbers, the first 3 digits divided by the last 2 digits equals 3.

For example 102 ÷ 34 = 3.

276 ÷ 69 = 4, not 3.

Find something in common in the following pairs of words.

stop —— chew

pore —— hark

cart —— take

oversee   knack
pelican   duty
legacy   edge
banish   allow
chief   ?

What word is missing from the second column?

Is it – immortal, peculiar, happy or indignant?

121 Answer

Swapping the first two letters of one of the words in each pair with the last two letters of the other word and vice versa spells out pairs of foodstuffs:

stop ——— chew
pore ——— hark
cart ——— take

122 Answer

indignant

Look at the end of each word in the first column and the beginning of the word opposite in the second column to find the saying: *seek and ye shall find*, i.e.

over(see   k)nack
pelic(an   d)uty
legac(y   e)dge
bani(sh   all)ow
chie(f   ind)ignant

Find the number that is three places away from itself doubled, two places away from itself plus 2, three places away from itself less 1, two places away from itself plus 3, three places away from itself less 3, and two places away from itself plus 6. Diagonal moves are allowed.

17	37	10	35	30	4	14
48	29	20	16	1	13	3
23	70	34	19	52	50	36
4	31	2	7	15	5	6
28	56	26	8	2	12	25
22	9	21	11	29	8	18

123 Answer

5.

Replace the question mark with the appropriate number.

	28	16			38	59			34	25	
47			59	25			38	28			?
		64				13				23	

Where would you place the missing letters L and M in the grid?

J	Q	C	T	K	F
B	U	N	Y	G	V
P	E		H	X	D
I	W			O	*
A	R			Z	S

124 Answer

3.

The three numbers in identical positions in each group add up to 100.

For example: 59 + 38 + 3 = 100.

125 Answer

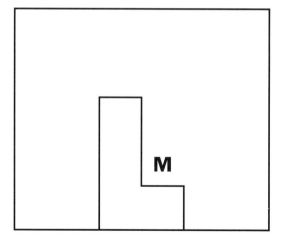

Which is the odd one out?

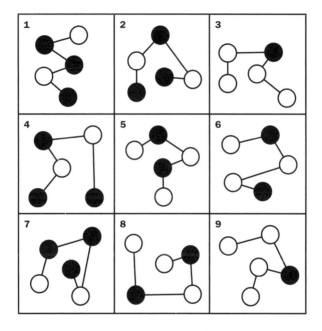

6.
1 and 7 contain the same string of circles, as do 2 and 4, 9 and 3, 5 and 8.

What do these words all have in common?

DREW
OIL
DEFT
RED
LOOK
DEFER
LOP

127 **Answer**

They can all be typed by moving to adjacent letters (including those diagonally adjacent) on a standard Qwerty keyboard.

Substitute letters for numbers to find five 5-letter words that are all anagrams of each other.

12345

21435

32145

43215

53214

128 Answer

Times, items, mites, emits, smite.

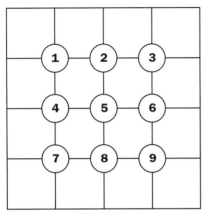

Clues:
1. Notion
2. Prepare book for publication
3. Story
4. Business transaction
5. Told untruth
6. Small island
7. Amphibious mammal with flippers
8. Thin
9. Fail to hit

The answers are all 4-letter words. Each one revolves either clockwise or anti-clockwise around its particular number. To further complicate matters, you have to figure out the starting point of each word.

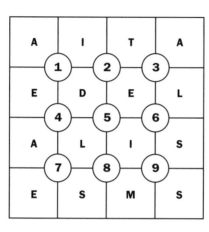

1. idea
2. edit
3. tale
4. deal
5. lied
6. isle
7. seal
8. slim
9. miss

shiver + noisy = hover
haven + cavity = taxing
onion + never = jovial

therefore:
hairy + brisk = ?

Choose from:
rowing, diving, boxing, skiing, or running

skiing
Take the Roman numeral value from the center of each word and add;
so that ha**i**ry + br**is**k = sk**ii**ng.
In the same way that sh**iv**er + no**is**y = ho**ver**

In each column just one set of letters can be arranged into a
5-letter English word. Can you find the two words?

MURTA	NUGAL
CRILD	IGTAP
UDECA	IAGWL
JAENO	MURDO
LOTBA	HIRDA
PHLEI	LEANF
CKUBL	WEOPN
AINTM	YENOL
CODAP	CIUTN
AQNLU	NEFCI

Column 1 LOTBA = bloat
Column 2 CIUTN = tunic

What 3-letter word should replace the question mark?

broke	cute
pump	evil
sung	egged
prose	rage
dared	lasses
bowl	?

Place the same digit twice into this sum to make it correct.

4　　　/　　　6　　　=　　　4

132 Answer

kin.
Pair a word from the first column with a word from the second column to obtain six compound words: brokerage, prosecute, bowlegged, sunglasses, daredevil and, finally, pumpkin.

133 Answer

4.

$4^4 / 64 = 4$

Twice six are eight of us,
But half six are seven of us,
Nine are but four of us,
So what can we be?

Want to know more of us?
We will tell more of us,
Twelve are but six of us,
One less is seven of us.

Now do you see?

134 **Answer**

The number of letters in the word/words;

i.e.   twice six = 8 letters

        half six = 7 letters

        nine = 4 letters

Use each letter once only in the following four phrases to spell out three of a kind.

a. Three countries:
   inside each billionaire

b. Three animals:
   rational ecology boob

c. Three trees:
   chose abbey ceremony

d. Three parts of the human body:
   he crushed skeleton

a. Indonesia, Liberia, Chile
b. gorilla, coyote, baboon
c. beech, ebony, sycamore
d. shoulder, knee, chest

Start with the central letter E, then move to another letter within the wheel, and continue jumping to alternate letters in a clockwise rotation to produce a quotation. Each letter is used only once. The problem is to find the next letter after E, and just to confuse matters there are nine missing letters, which can be arranged to spell out the originator of the quotation.

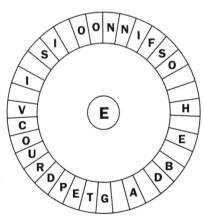

Education is the best provision for old age.

Aristotle

Timber! 137

If a man and a half can cut down a tree and a half in a hour and a half, how many trees can nine men cut down in nine hours?

Concert 138

The entire village turned out for a concert, 120 people attending and paying $120 altogether.

Tickets were priced : $5 adults
$2 over-65 year olds
10 cents children

How many adults, over 65s and children were there?

54.
One man can cut down 2/3 of a tree in one hour;
therefore, 9 men will cut down 6 trees in one hour;
and 54 men in 9 hours.

17 adults, 13 over-65s and 90 children.

How much are fruit bowls?

SHIRTS	$51
WRISTWATCHES	$93
PERFUME	$43
FOOD HAMPERS	$74
FRUIT BOWLS	?

Which is the only day of the week that has a certain feature in common with the months of March and May, and the astrological signs of Aries, Virgo, and Pisces?

139 Answer

$73.
In the spelling of fruit bowls there are 7 consonants and 3 vowels.

140 Answer

Monday.
It is the only one that will anagram into another English word (i.e. dynamo). The only months that will anagram are March = charm and May = yam. The only astrological signs that will anagram are Aries = raise, arise,
Virgo = vigor, and Pisces = spices.

Four explorers deep in the Amazon jungle have to cross a rope bridge in the middle of a moonless night. Unfortunately the bridge is only strong enough to support two people at a time. Also, because deep in the Amazon jungle on a moonless night it is pitch black dark, the explorers need a torch to guide them, otherwise there is every likelihood they would lose their footing and plunge to their deaths in the ravine below. However, between them they have only one torch.

Young Alec can cross the ravine in four minutes, his sister Maria can cross in 6 minutes, their father George can cross in 12 minutes. However, old Colonel Pipkins can only hobble across in 25 minutes.

How quickly is it possible for all four to reach the other side?

47 minutes.

first Alec and Maria cross	= 6 minutes
then Alec returns	= 4 minutes
then George and Col. Pipkins cross	= 25 minutes
then Maria returns	= 6 minutes
finally Alec and Maria return	= 6 minutes

What number should replace the question mark?

4	2	2	2
3	1	1	4
3	2	1	5
2	3	4	?

10.
Starting at 4 and working clockwise, the total of each diagonal line of numbers is 4, 5(2+3), 6(2+1+3), 7(2+1+2+2), etc.

Insert the 26 letters of the alphabet into the grid once each only to complete the crossword

143 Answer

N		S		E	J	E	C	T
A	X	I	S		A		O	
V		Z		Q	U	E	R	Y
A	B	E	T		N		K	
L		D	O	T	T	Y		K
	G		M		Y	A	W	N
G	L	O	A	T		C		I
	E		T		C	H	E	F
D	E	P	O	T		T		E

MINUET
TICKET
ENGINE
IGNORE
NATURE
    ?

What comes next?

tablet, autumn, unrest, priest, or statue

autumn.

The second word begins with the last letter of the first word, the third word begins with the fifth letter of the second word, the fourth word begins with the fourth letter of the third word, etc.

Insert the name of a major U.S. city in the third column reading downwards in order to complete ten 3-letter words reading across.

P	A	*
H	U	*
H	O	*
T	O	*
T	A	*
P	A	*
C	U	*
S	E	*
M	A	*
H	A	*

145 **Answer**

New Orleans.

Trace the chords across the circle to find letters that will spell out a manmade landmark. If the next letter is within 4 letters of the previous letter in the alphabet it will be traced along the circumference. Beware of a set of consecutive letters.

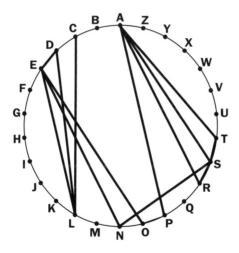

146 Answer

Cleopatra's Needle.

Find a reason for arranging these words into four groups of three words each.

ANT
COMFORT
DOWN
FEET
FRONT
HEAD
HEART
IT
PURSUIT
SEAT
SHOULDER
SPOT

comfort, feet, shoulder:
> All can be prefixed with cold.

seat, pursuit, head:
> All can be prefixed with hot.

front, heart, spot:
> All can be prefixed with warm.

down, it, ant:
> All can be prefixed with cool (coolant).

With the aid of the clues complete two magic word squares where the words read the same horizontally and vertically. There is also a bonus clue which leads to a 7-letter word that also appears both horizontally and vertically in the grid.

Clues (in no particular order):
First name of
  Miss Jean Baker
Approaches closely
To cause to accept
Wound caused by a nettle
Operatic male voice

Relating to a city
Keyed up
Relatively large in size
Concur
Provoke or deride

Bonus clue: elderly relative

S	T	I	N	G			
T	E	N	O	R			
I	N	U	R	E			
N	O	R	M	A			
G	R	E	A	T	A	U	N	T
				A	G	R	E	E
				U	R	B	A	N
				N	E	A	R	S
				T	E	N	S	E

1. liner
2. time
3. quarter
4. square
5. star
6. gun
7. ?

What comes next?
Is it balls, pins, seas, fingers, or halves?

seas.

One-liner, two-time, three-quarter, four-square, five-star, six-gun, seven-seas.

Delete three letters in each square to form a crossword that is made up in the usual way with interlocking seven-letter English words.

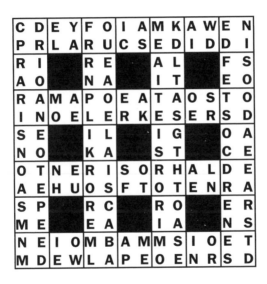

150 Answer

P	Y	R	A	M	I	D
O		E		A		E
I	M	P	R	E	S	S
N		L		S		C
T	H	I	S	T	L	E
E		C		R		N
D	I	A	M	O	N	D

NE : LIED
SE : MATI
SW : VUIH
NW : RYTE

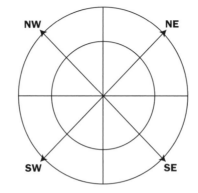

Place the letters in the correct boxes in each quadrant to obtain two related eight-letter words, one reading clockwise and one counter-clockwise.

151 Answer

relative, humidity.

What letter should replace the question mark?

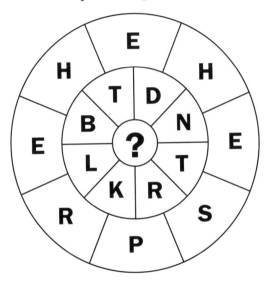

A.

So that each group of 4 letters (i.e. the central A with two adjacent letters on the inner wheel and one adjacent letter on the outer wheel) spell out a four-letter English word: hand, neat, star, park, lark, able, bath, and date.

Find the words and their containers below.
For example: meat in a river (3 letters inside 6 letters) =
T(ham)es

first man in a soothsayer (4 in 11)
insect in a written name (4 in 9)
middle-eastern country in a predatory fish (4 in 7)
mollusc in a flower (4 in 8)
nightbird in SE China port (3 in 7)
Shakespeare king in Mediterranean islands (4 in 8)
type of tree in someone who saw something for himself
    (3 in 3-7)
snake in a sea (3 in 7)
US city in a French city (4 in 8)
European capital in instrument of pressure (4 in 9)
cereal crop in muscles (4 in 7)
type of meat in beach party (4 in 8)

Nostr(adam)us
si(gnat)ure
p(iran)ha
cy(clam)en
K(owl)oon
Ba(lear)ic
e(ye-w)itness
c(asp)ian
G(reno)ble
ba(rome)ter
t(rice)ps
c(lamb)ake

What do all the following have in common, and which of them has a little more of it then the rest?

Arc de Triomphe

chemin de fer

hiccoughing

film noir

piano players

air-strikes

art students

They all contain three consecutive letters of the alphabet; however, film noir contains four—lmno.

Below are six piles of counters, each of the three piles on the
right contain an even number of counters and each of the
three piles on the left an odd number of counters.

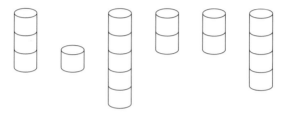

How many piles do you need to pick up so that the row of
counters contains alternate piles of even and odd counters?

155 Answer

Just one pile.
Pick up the pile of counters on the extreme right.
Drop one counter each on the first, third and fourth piles.

Swap two of the cards on the top row with two of the cards on the bottom row to form a fraction equalling one-sixth:

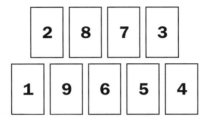

Now do the same below to form a fraction equalling one-eighth:

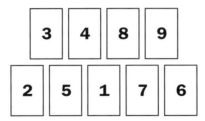

$$\frac{2943}{17658}$$

$$\frac{3187}{25496}$$

a. How many minutes is it before 1pm if 42 minutes ago it was 5 times as many minutes past 11am?

b. How many minutes is it before 12 noon if 24 minutes ago it was three times as many minutes past 10am?

c. How many minutes is it before 1pm if 30 minutes ago it was four times as many minutes past 9am?

Odd One Out 158

Which is the odd one out?

   The American Dream

   The Grand Canyon

   A Little Englander

   The Prodigal Son

   A Neanderthal Man

   The Ten Commandments

157 Answer

a. 13 minutes
b. 24 minutes
c. 42 minutes

158 Answer

The Prodigal Son. It contains the word ALSO –
The Prodig**al So**n

The rest contain the word AND:
The Americ**an D**ream
The G**rand** Canyon
A Little Engl**and**er
A Ne**and**erthal Man
The Ten Comm**and**ments

After a terrible start to the season, the local college soccer team had a great high scoring victory. The coach, who had a keen eye for statistics, suddenly noticed something very unusual.

"Look at our last ten scores!" he exclaimed. "Our first score indicates the number of times we have scored just one goal, our second score indicates the number of times we have scored 2, our third score indicates the number of times we scored 3, and, believe it or not, this carries on right up to our tenth score, which indicates the number of times we scored zero."

What were the scores in our last ten matches?

Answer

2100010006

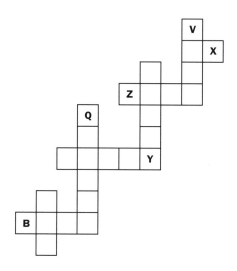

Using all of the 26 letters of the alphabet once each only complete the crossword.

Six letters have already been placed.

160 Answer

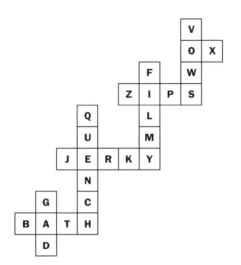

A palindrome reads the same backward or foreward.

Solve each anagram to find, in each case, a palindromic phrase.

For example: Dad, I am Mamma = Madam I'm Adam

a. real gargle
b. opponent's set
c. redden over oven
d. it awaits a swab
e. Soviet rioters
f. violent loser variants
g. as aimless masses fail
h. pre-eminent moron met Nemesis

a. regal lager
b. step on no pets
c. never odd or even
d. was it a bat I saw
e. rise to vote, sir
f. rats live on no evil star
g. ma is as selfless as I am
h. some men interpret nine memos

At the casino, gamblers were playing a game involving throwing two standard dice. I missed the first throw and asked the players the total of the two dice.
The following are the answers I received:

A. it was even 2 - 4 - 6 - 8 - 10 - 12
B. it was odd   1 - 3 - 5 - 7 - 9 - 11
C. it was a prime number 2 - 3- 5 - 7 - 11
D. it was a square number 1 - 4 - 9
E. it was 8 - 9 - 10 - 11 or 12

However, only one person was telling the truth.

Who was telling the truth, and what was the total?

 **Answer**

A told the truth—the answer is 6.

	A	B	C	D	E
1		x		x	
2	x		x		
3		x	x		
4	x			x	
5		x	x		
6	x				
7		x	x		
8	x				x
9		x		x	x
10	x				x
11		x	x		x
12	x				x

Answer 6 has one cross = one true answer

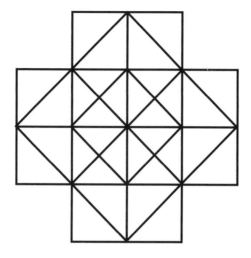

How many squares are there in this diagram?

163 Answer

27.

In the following, cross out the superfluous letters to leave a sentence that makes sense.

    ATSHENETSUEPEN
    CERTFLHAUOTUMSA
    KELESTSTENERSES

Heteronyms are a word or words that are spelled alike but sound different, for example, *onus* and *on us*.
In each of the following rewrite the sentence substituting in each case a pair of homonyms.
For example, the sentence *The burden was not our responsibility* could be rewritten *The **onus** was not **on us***.

i) I moved the large book in my direction
ii) It was the time of the year for the navel boy
iii) The staff were coping with the male's advancing years
iv) The lady's piece of jewelry had been swallowed by the fish
v) The most serious people moved the large marble slabs

164 Answer

Cross out *the superfluous letters* to leave *a sentence that makes sense*

A**T**SHE**N**E**TS**UE**P**EN
CE**RT**F**L**HA**UO**TU**MS**A
KE**LEST**S**T**ENE**RS**ES

165 Answer

i) I moved the tome to me
ii) It was the season for the sea son
iii) The staff were managing with the man aging
iv) Her ring had been swallowed by the herring
v) The gravest ones moved the gravestones.

Find a trite saying, known as Ornstein's Law, in which all the vowels have been removed, and the consonants arranged into five groups.

In each group the letters are in the correct order, however, the groups are not in the correct order.

For example, FIND THE TRITE SAYING could appear TRTSY NG FNDTH.

SGNTH CDG NBDYV TSYSN RPTST

Nobody ever puts out a sign that says nice dog.

Which four of the six pieces can be fitted together to form a perfect square?

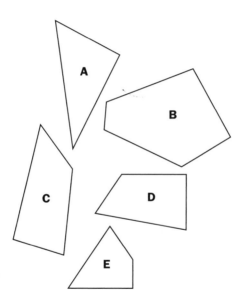

167 Answer

ABDE

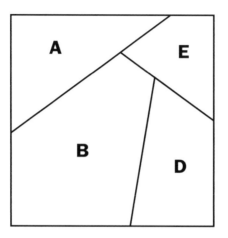

Apart from all ending in the letter E what do all these words have in common?

care

joke

cake

fore

rebuke

They are all made up of the first two letters of the names of post-World War II U.S. Presidents:

CA = Carter
RE = Reagan
JO = Johnson
KE = Kennedy
FO = Ford
BU = Bush

Complete the following hyphenated words, all of which appear in Webster's 10th Dictionary. The number of dots indicates the number of missing letters.

..TY - FR..

...ST - CA..

....ER - PA....

..OT - CH...

..RD - PR.....

...ET - FO....

...ID - LO.....

.EE - HA.

...AD - SP......

....LE - CL...

.....OW - TA....

...EY - SP.....

..AR - UL.........

..RM - EA...

....IE - TA....

.....ED - AC....

...SE - PA.....

..TA - RE......

duty-free
worst-case
pitter-patter
spot-check
hard-pressed
fleet-footed
solid-looking
hee-haw
broad-spectrum
middle-class
swallow-tailed
money-spinner
near-ultraviolet
worm-eaten
walkie-talkie
limited-access
passe-partout
beta-receptor

Where would you logically place number 5 in the grid?

7							9
							3
							1
			2		4	
				6		
8							

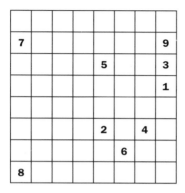

With odd numbers start at the top left-hand corner and work along the top line then back across the second line etc., counting empty squares before inserting the first odd number (i.e. count nine empty squares then insert 9 in the ninth square, then seven empty squares and insert 7 in the seventh square etc.) With even numbers do the same but start at the bottom right-hand square.

Divide the square into four parts of equal size and shape.
Each part must contain the same 9-letters that can be
arranged to spell out a 9-letter English word.

O	U	G	N	G	N
N	C	R	R	T	E
T	R	O	C	C	G
N	E	N	U	O	U
E	C	G	O	R	N
N	T	U	E	T	N

congruent

O	U	G	N	G	N
N	C	R	R	T	E
T	R	O	C	C	G
N	E	N	U	O	U
E	C	G	O	R	N
N	T	U	E	T	N

Replace letters with numbers to solve this addition sum:

MARS
VENUS
URANUS
<u>SATURN</u>
NEPTUNE

i) What is the longest English word that can be produced from the following ten letters?

MUERVHANYL

ii) What is the longest English word that can be produced from the following ten letters?

NURDESBOTA

172 Answer

$$4593$$
$$20163$$
$$695163$$
$$\underline{358691}$$
$$1078610$$

173 Answer

i) humanely

ii) eastbound

Each arrangement of letters represents a word or phrase.

i) O_{ted}

ii) g**AG**ged

iii) PR
     B

iv) **AVI**

174 **Answer**

i) bigoted
ii) silence is golden
iii) proverb
iv) center of gravity

Each of the following is an anagram of a well-known phrase. The number of letters in the phrase is indicated in parentheses.

    a. heated tray (2,3,5)
    b. brand old horse (2,5,6)
    c. count doses (7,3)
    d. it reaches envy (5,4,4)
    e. demolition gal (3,2,4,4)
    f. heigh-ho! to warmer cell (4,4,2,4,5)
    g. it is the arch bogey-man (7,6,2,4)
    h. the woody generator room (4,5,4,8)

a. at the ready
b. no holds barred
c. seconds out
d. seven year itch
e. all in good time
f. come hell or high water
g. charity begins at home
h. here today gone tomorrow

COUNT

AREA

DEUCE

TRADE

NOTE

ARID

Which word does not belong in the sequence?

Trade.
The words repeat the consonants CNTRD in the same order.

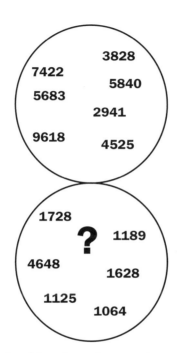

What number should replace the question mark?

2320.

Multiply the two halves of all the numbers in the top circle to obtain the numbers in the bottom circle, i.e. 74x22=1628, 38x28=1064, 56x83=4648, 29x41=1189, 96x18=1728, 45x25=1125; which leaves 58x40=2320.

What is the longest word you can find by moving from letter to letter horizontally, vertically, or diagonally and not repeat a letter?

L	E	S	O
B	U	N	D
A	A	E	R
D	N	T	S

 **Answer**

Understandable.

Sue, Sam, and Sally are taking part in an archery contest. So far they have hit the target 29 times between them as indicated below. Sally has scored a third more than Sam, and Sam has scored a third more than Sue. Altogether they have scored 185.

How many has each scored and what are their individual hits?

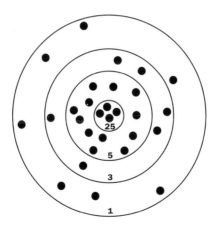

Sue 45: 1 x25, 3 x 5, 1 x 3, 2 x 1
Sam 60: 1 x 25, 3 x 5, 5 x 3, 5 x 1
Sally 80 : 2 x 25, 6 x 5

In the final circuit of the Indianapolis 500 just ten cars are left in the race, the leader being car number 5, followed by car 4. At the rear of the field is car number 3. What logically should be the number of the car next to last?

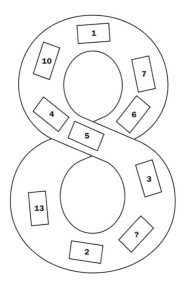

Car 14.

The sum of each pair of cars increases by 2 from first to last, i.e. 5 + 4 = 9, 10 + 1 = 11, 7 + 6 = 13, 13 + 2 = 15, and 14 + 3 = 17.

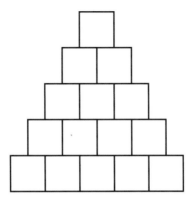

Complete the pyramid with 1 x one letter, 1 x two letter, 1 x three letter, 1 x four letter, and 1 x five letter words. The 15-letters when correctly inserted can be arranged to spell out a 15-letter word.

Clues: the chemical symbol for sulphur (1)

refers to a non-human or inanimate thing (2)

tree of the genus Ulmus (3)

engage in games (4)

sailing vessel (5)

S, it, elm, play, yacht
15-letter word = sympathetically

Start at the center * and work from letter to adjacent letter horizontally, vertically, and diagonally to spell out six words. Five of the words are synonyms of CAPABLE, however, one of the words is an antonym of CAPABLE. Finish at the top right-hand square and visit every square once each only.

L	P	M	C	E	P	T
I	H	E	O	C	D	A
S	S	D	A	T	E	T
P	L	K	*	E	O	N
R	U	I	L	P	M	C
F	O	F	E	N	E	T
I	C	I	T	I	N	P

accomplished
skilful
proficient
inept (antonym)
competent
adept

SUNDAY
MONDAY
TUESDAY
WEDNESDAY
THURSDAY
FRIDAY
SATURDAY

What day immediately follows the day that comes three days before the day that comes immediately before the day which comes two days after the day that comes three days before the day which comes midway between the day two days after Thursday and the day immediately following Wednesday?

183 Answer

Monday.

Jack and Jill went up the hill to fetch some water to fill their tub. After the tub was filled Jack said, "I can't remember how many pails of water we brought in." "I remember," said Jill, "it was less than 100, and if you double the number and add one, then divide that by three, add one and double that number again, we get the reverse of the number."

"You mean like 26 and 62?"

"That's right, but those two numbers are not correct," said Jill.

Jack couldn't figure it out.

How many pails of water did they bring?

46.

The name Carolina can be produced from the letters of California and the name Kansas is contained in another state—Arkansas. However, can you figure out the following:

The name Maine can be produced from the names of which two other states? From one of these other states can also be produced the name of a middle east country and also this county's former name. From the name of the other state from which Maine can be produced, can also be produced the name of an Eastern European state, a middle east Sultanate, an ancient civilization, and a French painter. How many can you name?

The name Utah can be produced from the names of which two other states? From one of these other states can also be produced the name of the capital of the middle east Sultanate mentioned above, and a famous river in England. How many of these can you name?

Maine can be produced from New Hampshire, from which can be produced Iran and Persia; and Minnesota, from which can be produced Estonia, Oman, Minoan, and Monet.

Utah can be produced from South Carolina and Massachusetts, from which can also be produced Muscat (the capital of Oman) and Thames.

It is only possible to arrange the letters of the word

EYE

in three possible ways so that the same arrangement of letters does not appear (i.e EYE, EEY and YEE).
In how many different ways is it possible to arrange the letters in the word

MONOPOLY

so that the same arrangement of letters does not appear?

13440

$$8! = \frac{8 \times 7 \times 6 \times 5 \times 4 \times 3 \times 2 \times 1}{3}$$

Using the word CAT, for example, to solve this type of puzzle, you use 3!, which means factorized 3 (i.e. 3 x 2 x 1 = 6), when all of the letters are different. If a letter repeats, for example A and another A, then divide the answer by 2.
If a letter is trebled in any position then divide by 3, as in the word monopoly, which uses three Os.

What weight must be placed at the ? to balance the scale?

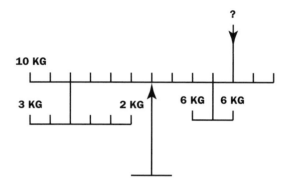

11kg.

10 x 6 = 60	12 x 3 = 36
5 x 4 = <u>20</u>	11 x 4 = <u>44</u>
80	80

Explanation:

Left-hand side—lower balance 3 x 2 = 2 x 3 (so balances). Added together represents a weight at main scale of 5kg pressure.

So:

Left-hand side =	Right-hand side =
10 x 6 = 60	12 x 3 = 36
5 x 4 = <u>20</u>	11 x 4 = <u>44</u>
80 Balances	80

Solve the four rebuses below. Each represents a familiar phrase.

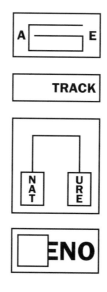

middle-age spread
on the right track
balance of nature
back to square one